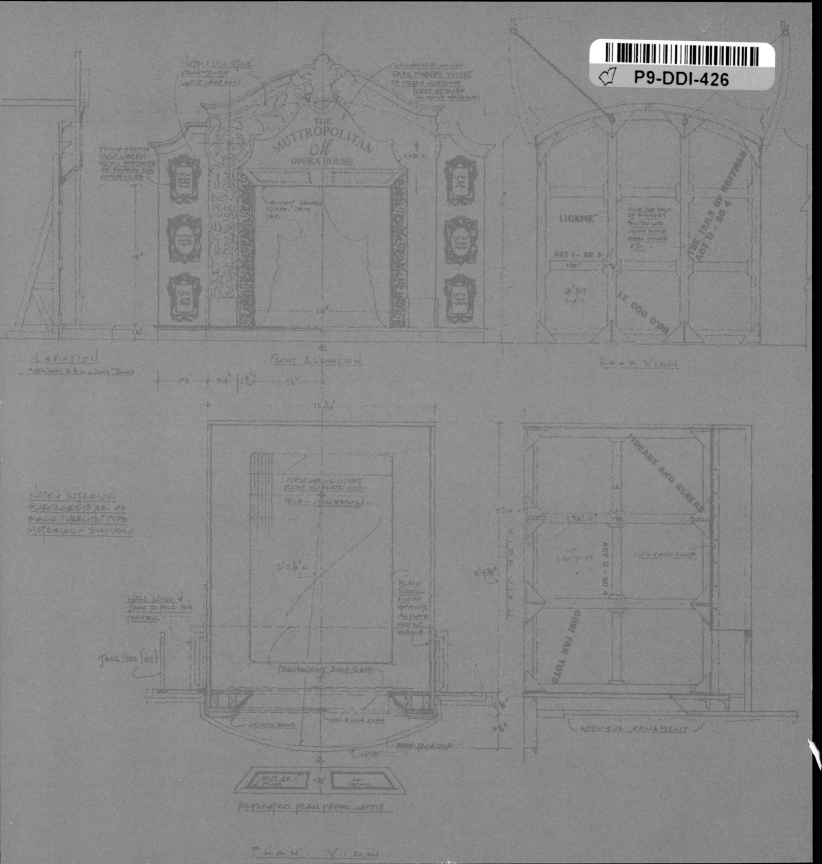

BARKITECTURE

BARKITECTURE

by Fred Albert

Abbeville Press Publishers
New York • London

For Murphy

FRONT COVER: The Stella Dome. See p. 21.

BACK COVER (clockwise from top left):
House for a Modernist Mutt, see p. 48;
Dog Cabin, see p. 68; 1880 Doghouse from Bangor,
Maine, see p. 10; Foreign Correspondent, see p. 53.

ENDPAPERS: Plans for the Muttropolitan
Opera House. See p. 81.

PAGES 1 AND 96: The Trojan Dog. See p. 75.

PAGE 2: Budapet. See p. 44.

PAGE 3: Let Sleeping Dogs Lie. See p. 58.

PAGE 6: Drawing of Garden Pavillion
for Dave. See p. 83.

Contents

Introduction

If recent findings are correct, the bond between man and dog dates back 100,000 years or more. Which suggests that somewhere between the Ice Age and the Bronze Age, man built the first doghouse.

The urge to fashion a home for our pets seems as innate as the desire to dress them in jaunty vests or feed them free-range kibble. And makes about as much sense. (Have you ever seen a dog wash down a gourmet meal with toilet water?) As Ralph Caplan observed in his amusing, insightful catalog accompanying a doghouse exhibit at the Cooper-Hewitt National Design Museum in New York, "Doghouses are not so much designed for dogs as for the owners of dogs." True, indeed. How else to explain the glorious cavalcade of exotic, elaborate, and downright whimsical canine casas gracing these pages? We project on our pets the same desires that we, ourselves, subscribe to—one of them being the desire to live in a really cool house. Most of us can't achieve that for ourselves. But we *can* do it for our dogs.

(One notable exception: Marie Antoinette, who kept a *niche à chien* at Versailles—an *extremely* cool house. Her doghouse—one of the few surviving from this period—was fabricated from wood and upholstered with turquoise silk held in place by brass-headed nails. The top was fitted with a removable domed lid to facilitate cleaning. After all, who do you think got to eat all that leftover cake?)

Around this same time, in 1788, the Earl Bishop of Derry commissioned a pair of canine residences from the (as-yet-unknighted) architect John Soane. The Englishman supplied designs for a residence of a canine family in both modern and ancient styles, featuring three wings radiating out from a domed atrium.

Slightly less ambitious was the early-nineteenth-century French doghouse that now resides at Washington Irving's landmark home in upstate

Marie Antoinette's *niche à chien,*
mid-eighteenth century

New York. Although the author of *Rip Van Winkle* never used this piece, it's still quite charming, with decorative barge boards and a trefoil-shaped cresting along the top that mimics the Gothic Revival style then in vogue. Another Gothic Revival doghouse survives in Bangor, Maine, where it was built in 1880 to mimic the look of the main house (a practice still common today).

Dogs have been a mainstay of the nation's first families from the time of George Washington. The White House grounds have seen numerous kennels and the occasional doghouse over the years, including ones for Benjamin Harrison in the 1880s and Dwight D. Eisenhower in the 1950s. Lyndon Johnson was especially particular about his doghouse, insisting on numerous improvements, including heat, floodlights, and a Dutch door so LBJ could pet the dogs without releasing them. (He was not so particular about his training methods, earning the ire of dog lovers every-

Introduction

where when he was photographed picking up his beagles by their ears.)

It was during the presidency of Ronald Reagan that the idea of doghouse-as-status-symbol became popular, boosted by a puckish parody of *Vogue* called *Dogue*. The magazine included a roundup of some of the world's most stylish doggy digs, including Chinese dog pagodas and canine Cotswold cottages. In 1988 the Atlanta Humane Society hosted an exhibit of designer doghouses called *Architectural Dogfest,* and in 1989 the Kentucky Art and Craft Gallery followed suit with *Going to the Dogs: Shelter for the Discerning Canine.* The following year, the Cooper-Hewitt (a division of the Smithsonian Institution) exhibited two dozen architect-designed doghouses in their garden. The show earned mountains of publicity for both the museum and the exhibit's beneficiary, Guiding Eyes for the Blind, Inc., and launched a seemingly endless stream of charity doghouse competitions (from which many of the examples in this book were chosen).

Early-nineteenth-century doghouse at Sunnyside, the Washington Irving Estate in upstate New York

Bangor, Maine, doghouse from 1880

Not every doggy sweater gets worn, and not every doghouse gets used. But in the end—to borrow from Ralph Caplan—doghouses aren't really for dogs. Doghouses give dog owners the opportunity to express their love for their pets—to repay these animals for the loyalty and companionship they show us every day. It's a tall order. But a really cool house is a good start.

Introduction

Poster from Atlanta Humane Society designer doghouse exhibit, 1988

Detail of House of Coco. See page 28.

Putting on the Dog

Inspired by the architecture of the past but designed for the doggy of today, every one of these houses is a miniature work of art. From a pint-sized château in Florida to a conical Craftsman in California, each exhibits a mastery of details and materials worthy of MUTTROPOLITAN HOME or BARKITECTURAL DIGEST.

Chessie's Doghouse
John M. Collins
Locust Valley, New York

This exquisite English timber frame doghouse was modeled after an eighty-year-old children's playhouse on Long Island. The antique, hand-hewn beams are held in place with mortise-and-tenon joints, and are topped with an authentic thatch roof. Antique glass fills the custom-made windows, which are held in place by bone-shaped latches. A matching leash holder flanks the front door.

Jordan Saunders and her husband, Thomas A. Saunders III, installed the doghouse at their Long Island home. "Every spring we put flowers in the window boxes," says Jordan. "And we move it from time to time: My husband wanted to make sure it's always where it gets the best sun."

Château du Chien
Norman Sandler
Seattle

Architect Norman Sandler gets design credit for his Château du Chien, but it was his Samoyed, Wicket, that supplied the inspiration.

When Sandler volunteered to design a doghouse for a charity auction, it was Wicket's vaunted place in the Sandler household that suggested the notion of a temple. Turning to classical Greek architecture, Sandler designed a three-by-three-foot structure adorned with faux-marble columns and a copper roof. Clerestory windows inscribed with the names of famous dogs illuminate the interior, which features a granite floor and an inlaid Indian prayer rug. The stained-glass image of a doggy deity presides over the hand-blown water dish.

⯅ Canine/Bone
Order of Architecture
Terry Russell, Michael Donahue,
Ann Di Salvo
Louisville, Kentucky

Inspired by Benjamin Henry Latrobe's "three orders of architecture," architect Terry Russell and woodworker Michael Donahue devised their own: the "canine" order of architecture. The pair's interpretation of a classic Greek temple features plastic laminate walls, a fur-lined interior and cow bones in lieu of Ionic columns (making them, perhaps, *ironic* columns?).

As a crowning touch, artist Ann Di Salvo etched a frieze into the front pediment. Look closely and you'll see a man tossing a Frisbee to his dogs.

French Château ⯈
Hely Lima
Fort Lauderdale, Florida

Brazilian-born artist Hely Lima is known for his three-dimensional constructions depicting New York cityscapes. So naturally, when it came time to build a doghouse for his beloved West Highland terrier, Coco, no ordinary structure would do.

Coco's Florida home boasts a flip-top roof (for easy access and egress) and scored cardboard walls, which Lima painted by hand to simulate the mottled look of brick. Windows on each side encourage cross-ventilation, while wheels allow the doghouse to be moved from room to room.

The
Stella Dome
Barbara K. Westover
Oakland

In 1991 wildfires swept through Oakland, claiming thousands of homes, including that of architectural designer Barbara K. Westover and her husband, Christopher. Also lost was the three-story doghouse Westover had built for her mutt, Waylon.

Waylon never lived to see his doghouse rebuilt. But his successor, a yellow Lab named Stella, benefited from Westover's construction experience. Her stylish Craftsman doghouse (modeled after conical Italian houses called *trulli*) was built from scrap two-by-fours bound together like the staves of a barrel. The walls were stuccoed and topped with a slate roof (leftovers from the construction of Westover's new house) and a weathervane adorned with stars (for *Stella*, naturally).

◁ Villa Buster
Ralph L. Duesing
Dallas

Located across a stream and just uphill from Paul and Dody Wood's Dallas estate, this picturesque doghouse is often mistaken for an old pump house or garden folly.

In truth, it was built just a few years ago, along with the rest of the Woods' nine-thousand-square-foot home, using leftover limestone, slate, copper flashing, and a 350-pound cast-stone finial (supported by a steel frame.)

The proposed resident, a Rottweiler named Buster, turns up his nose at this canine citadel, preferring the comfort of the air-conditioned kennel, with its piped-in music and Dody Wood's organic, low-fat dog food.

"It's a food that even *I* can eat," Dody proclaims. "In fact, I *do*."

⌃ Hawaiian Doghouse
Jarrett Hedborg
Los Angeles

When the Los Angeles chapter of PAWS (Pets Are Wonderful Support) asked interior designer Jarrett Hedborg to design a fantasy doghouse, his mind naturally drifted to his favorite vacation spot, Hawaii.

With its bamboo columns, symmetrical palm-frond roof and wraparound porch, Hedborg's creation is fairly faithful to the traditional Hawaiian *hale*. (Except, of course, for the artificial rocks and Fortuny drapes.)

A towering palm tree anchors one corner of the doghouse, which is lined with tatami mats and decorated with tiki gods "to ward off evil fleas."

The Capitol Hill Doghouse
Doug Kelbaugh
Oysterville, Washington

Architect Doug Kelbaugh modeled this doghouse after the venerable bungalows populating his Seattle neighborhood. Although the wainscoting, belt course, and roof braces are pure Craftsman style, he took some liberties with the tail-shaped ridge beam and anthropomorphic feet.

Owner Polly Friedlander liked the way the extended front porch provided protection in rainy Northwest weather, and decided to add this doghouse to the other two she maintains for her fox terrier, Elmo.

"Of course, he doesn't *sleep* in them," she adds, slyly. "He sleeps in the house."

The Upper Canada Doghouse
John Bowron
Toronto

Architect John Bowron modeled his doghouse after the Sharon Temple of the Children of Peace, an early-nineteenth-century Quaker meetinghouse in Sharon, Ontario. Now it's home to Robin and Friday, an energetic pair of beagles belonging to Peter Carroll and U-Wen Kok of Toronto.

If the dogs took the time to look, they'd notice how Bowron provided them with a louvered cupola for ventilation and leaded-glass windows for light. And yes, that's copper flashing on the roof and a brass finial on top

The
House of Coco
Hely Lima
New York

When he's not lounging in his Florida château (see page 18), Coco retreats to Manhattan, where this pampered West Highland terrier receives guests in his very own Roman temple.

Built by owner Hely Lima, the doghouse is adorned with marbleized columns and lacy balustrades made from greeting-card trimmings. The dome on top is an inverted salad bowl painted gold.

Putting on the Dog

House for a Modernist Mutt. See page 48.

II

Modern Barkitecture

Forget Mies van der Rohe. Forget Le Corbusier. When it comes to cutting-edge design, those guys had nothing on this crew. The doghouses in this chapter represent an exquisite fusion of line, form, and function—each one guaranteed to put the BOW-WOW back into Bauhaus.

Château Neuf de Pup
Stuart Silk
Seattle

Ken Frankel's friends know that in most matters, his Alaskan malamute, Okuma, comes first. "She's sort of my primary relationship," laughs Ken.

So few are surprised to see Okuma's living quarters: a mock Parthenon that looks like a Lego model set within a framework of two-by-fours. The architect, Stuart Silk, says he was interested in contrasting the slick, colorful interior box with its primitive glass-roofed shell.

And what about Okuma? What does she think of her new home?

"She's always been somewhat reluctant to go inside," says Ken. Her master wasn't so timid. "The first time it showed up," he grins, "I crawled inside to check it out."

Modern Barkitecture

Red Rover

G. Phillip Smith, Smith and Thompson Architects
New York

Designed for a charitable auction in tony East Hampton, Long Island, this doghouse was based on the observation that dogs like to sit under and on top of things, not always inside. Architect G. Phillip Smith's tri-level structure features a shady retreat on the ground level and a sunny roof deck on top. The elevated interior is designed to be cool in summer and warm in winter. The stairs in back lead to a pool; a contoured channel in the roof replenishes the water every time it rains.

"We felt the dog should have a pool," Smith confides. "It *is* East Hampton."

Modern Barkitecture

The Dog Tower
Glenn Easley,
Benjamin Parco, NBBJ
San Francisco

Created for San Francisco radio personality
Don Bleu and his late keeshond, Lola, this
doghouse stands twelve feet high and features
an aluminum tower topped by a pair of
motion-activated spotlights. A counterweight
holds the hinged facade upright, forming a
shady canopy in front.

"My boss bought it and presented it
to me in the driveway one day," says Bleu,
whose resume includes a stint as host of
TV's *Gong Show*.

The doghouse was created by architectural designers Glenn Easley and Benjamin
Parco of NBBJ, who ended up having to
remove an office window and lower the piece
to the sidewalk in order to deliver it.

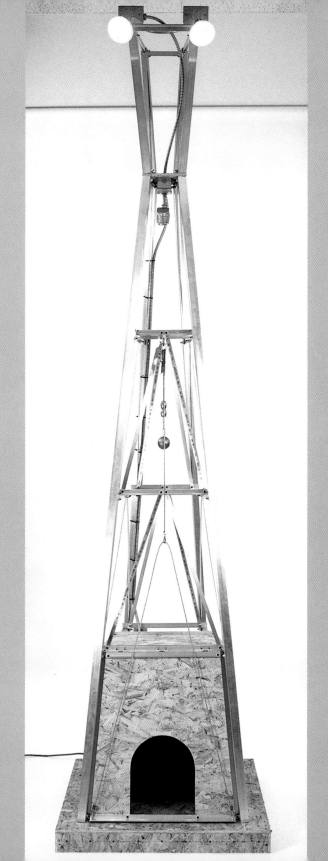

35

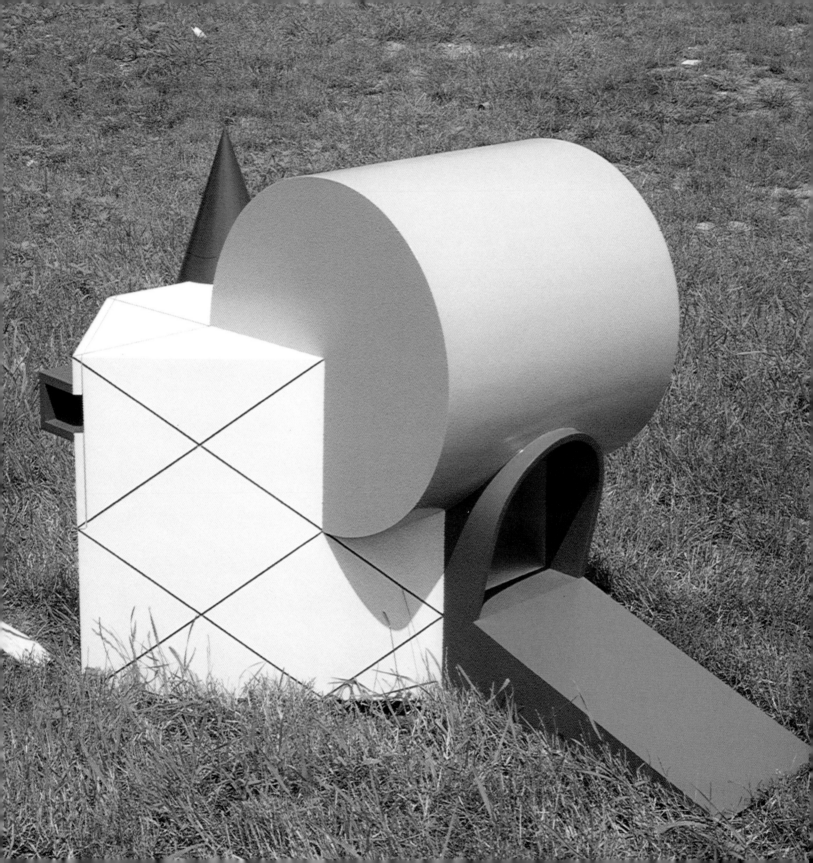

Villa Dog
Charles Gwathmey
New York

This colorful collision of geometric forms sprang from the fertile imagination of Charles Gwathmey of Gwathmey Siegel & Associates, whose high-profile commissions have included the addition to the Guggenheim Museum in New York.

Until recently, however, Gwathmey's resume was missing one thing: a really good doghouse. Fortunately, that oversight has been rectified with the completion of this Cubist creation. Built out of painted plywood, it includes windows and an integrated vent to admit light and air. The yellow panel inscribed with diamonds swings open to facilitate cleaning.

The Stealth Doghouse
Antoine Predock, Douglas L. Friend
Beverly Hills, California

Snoopy might have had better luck fighting the Red Baron had he been piloting one of these.

Modeled after the actual stealth bomber, the Stealth Doghouse features a stock plywood doghouse shell augmented with fiberglass-and-polyester-resin wings. Douglas L. Friend of Antoine Predock Architect in Venice, California, says the project was a natural outgrowth of the firm's interest in science fiction, high technology . . . and fun.

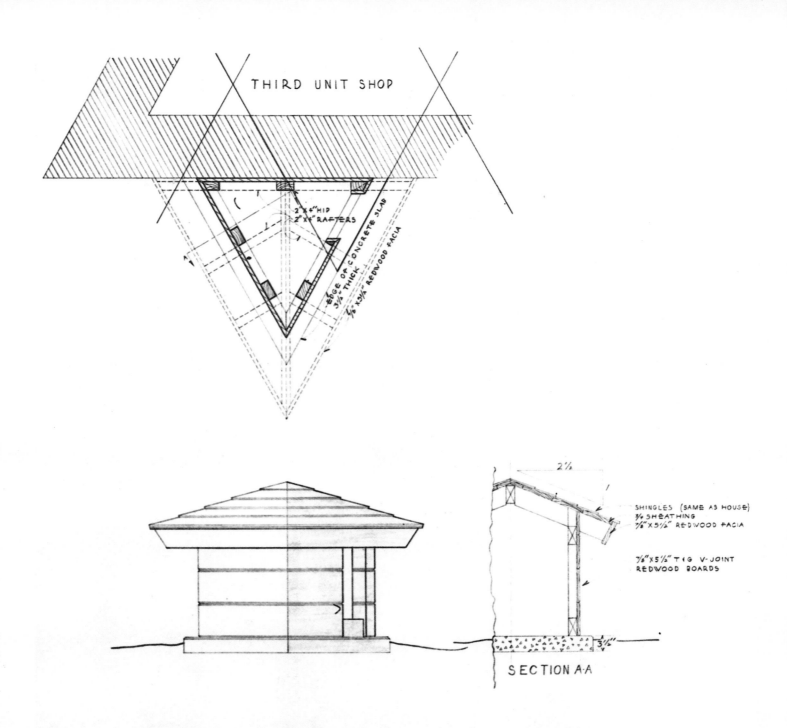

THIRD UNIT SHOP

2"x 4" HID
2"x 4" RAFTERS

EDGE OF CONCRETE SLAB
3/4" THICK

7/8" X 5½" REDWOOD FACIA

2½"

SHINGLES (SAME AS HOUSE)
3/8 SHEATHING
7/8" X 5½" REDWOOD FACIA

7/8" X 5½" T & G V-JOINT
REDWOOD BOARDS

3½"

SECTION A·A

Eddie's House
Frank Lloyd Wright
San Anselmo, California

In 1950 Frank Lloyd Wright designed a house near San Francisco for Robert and Gloria Berger. Six years later, their son, Jim, wrote to Wright and asked him to design a matching doghouse for his Labrador retriever, Eddie.

The architect responded nine days later, telling the youngster he would attend to the doghouse when he wasn't so busy. "Write me next November," Wright suggested, "and I may have something then."

On November 1, young Berger sent another letter to Wright. This time, the architect responded with a set of plans for a triangular doghouse designed to echo the motifs in the Bergers' Usonian-style home.

"The American Institute of Architects has nominated seventeen Frank Lloyd Wright buildings for preservation as outstanding contributions to American culture," notes Wright scholar Bruce Brooks Pfeiffer. "The Berger doghouse is not one of them."

Modern Barkitecture

Modern Barkitecture

The All-Seeing "Eye" Doghouse
Paul Haigh
Greenwich, Connecticut

Guide dogs don't use doghouses, since their duties require them to remain by their master's side. That didn't stop architect Paul Haigh from fashioning one anyway, equipped with a host of features designed to engage a visually impaired owner.

The aromatic cedar doghouse rests atop a platform set within an exterior armature (topped by an omniscient-looking eye). When a dog climbs up the ramp and steps inside the doghouse, the motion activates a chorus of chimes hanging underneath, alerting the owner to the dog's whereabouts. Side flaps labeled with the Braille symbols for eyes, ears, leg, and paw enable the owner to reach in and pet the animal. Another flap in back provides the dog with access to a water dish.

Budapet
John E. Holey, Greg Keffer, Jim Counts, Hal Tangen
San Francisco

Marcus and Jennifer Smith are the proud parents of a vizsla named Zipper. A relative of the weimaraner, vizslas originated in Hungary, which did not endear them to the Nazis, who tried to have the breed exterminated.

As a tribute to Zipper's heritage, architects and designers at Holey Associates in San Francisco designed the Budapet— a roving doghouse on wheels. The piece features a ribbed glass front and louvered back, with a gangplank that doubles as a door.

Zipper really uses the doghouse, as do the Smiths, who removed the wheels and turned the box into a side table.

⌃ Growler's Grove
Mark Millett
Oysterville, Washington

Inspired by the slatted-wood coyote fences he'd observed in the Southwest, Seattle architect Mark Millett fashioned his own version using undulating ribbons of sheet metal topped by a corrugated-steel roof. Willow branches or bamboo stalks could be trained to grow up through the slats, forming a living wall around the dog.

Owner Polly Friedlander inserted bamboo poles as an interim measure, but her fox terrier Elmo remains aloof, preferring his more traditional doghouse (see pages 24–25).

"He's not quite as avant-garde as I am," sighs Friedlander.

Bird/Dog House ⌵
Michael J. Brolly
Hamburg, Pennsylvania

After crafting a wooden bowl on a lathe, sculptor Michael J. Brolly realized that if he cut the piece into sections and assembled them correctly, the result might look like a dog-sized version of the Sydney Opera House.

Since Brolly's springer spaniel, Rosebud, is fond of birds, he added a turned-wood birdhouse under the eaves. Deciding to carry the Australian theme a little further, he decorated the interior with primitive imagery inspired by Aboriginal cave paintings.

"You know," Brolly asserts, "dogs need art, too."

Modern Barkitecture

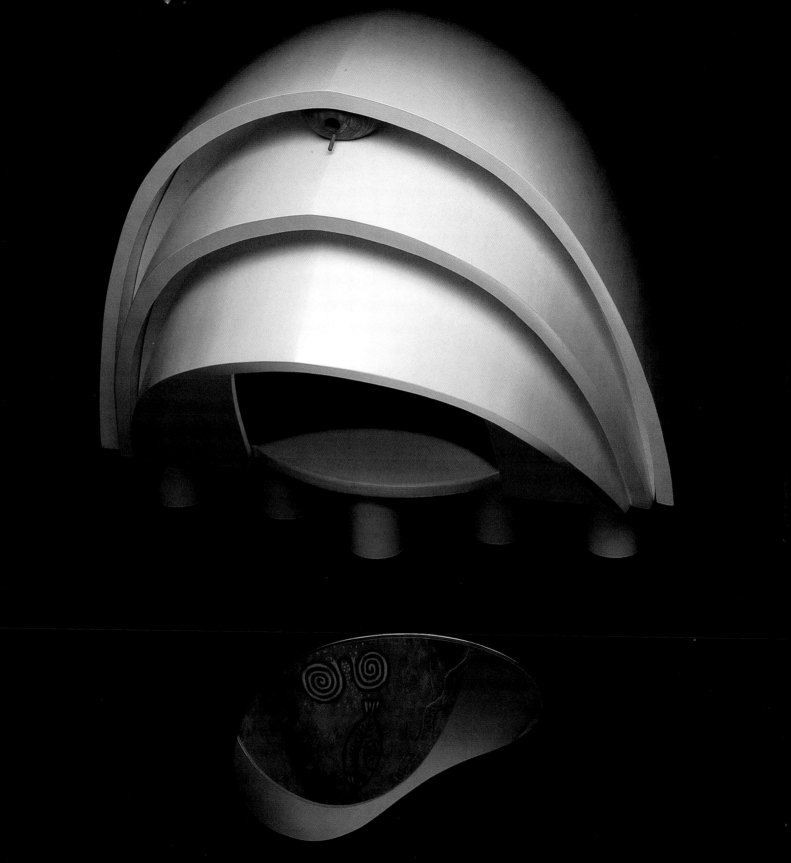

◁House for a Modernist Mutt
Virginia Senior, Jeff Oesterle
Phoenix

This minimalist marriage of Plexiglas and powder-coated steel was designed by architect Virginia Senior and metal sculptor Jeff Oesterle. Not for the bashful, the doghouse is equipped with a perforated-steel floor that's raised off the ground to encourage air circulation (and comparisons to Le Corbusier's Villa Savoie, no doubt).

Untitled No. 2▷
BWBR Architects
Saint Paul

Working in what he calls a "metaphorical, not deconstructivist" style, architectural designer Michael Meehan and five cohorts devised this cutting-edge doghouse, which they dubbed Untitled No. 2 (because it was their second idea).

They covered a trapezoidal pine shell with a bowed steel roof, then sliced off the side with a pair of skewed plywood wedges painted scarlet. The wall opposite the entry is fitted with a transparent plastic panel, affording protection from the elements while still allowing the dog to enjoy the view.

"Hopefully the dog isn't going to come running through and smash into that Plexiglas," muses Meehan.

If so, there's always Untitled No. 3.

Modern Barkitecture

Fido's Amazing Technicolor Dreamhouse. See page **68**.

III

A Breed Apart

There's no dogma here. The designers of these doghouses are all free thinkers, who looked to some unusual sources—a purse, a box of dog biscuits, an abandoned TV—for inspiration. The results are strictly one of a kind. For canines who like to stand out from the pack.

Foreign Correspondent
Babey Moulton Jue & Booth
San Francisco

Perfect for the pooch who likes to travel in style, this combination doghouse and sedan chair comes equipped with two carrying handles (humans not included).

The rococo exterior is topped with leafy fronds and a gold finial. Inside, there's plush upholstered seating and a bulletin board (to display postcards, no doubt). The Roman shades raise and lower, for the modest traveler who doesn't like drawing attention to himself.

◁ Doggy Bag
Stefan Hastrup
San Francisco

Invited to dream up a doghouse for San Francisco society columnist Pat Steger, architect Stefan Hastrup devised this oversized handbag on wheels.

Crafted from counterfeit patent leather (quilted on the diagonal for that chi-chi Chanel look), the doghouse is equipped with a set of bicycle buggy wheels and a carrying strap fabricated from a leather steering-wheel cover. When Steger's cockapoo, Jo Jo, gets bored, the dog can gaze at Steger's columns lining the interior. Or peer through the extendable magnifying glass—designed to help our intrepid reporter (and pet) penetrate every pocket of Bay Area society.

Niche à Chien ▷
Robert Vasseur
Louviers, France

Over the course of nearly half a century, Robert Vasseur has transformed his home and grounds into one of the most celebrated works of environmental folk art in France. Mosaics fashioned from seashells and colorful shards of crockery adorn nearly every inch of the retired milkman's home and garden.

Integrated into this suburban wonderland is an enchanting, mosaic-covered doghouse. Vasseur outlined the structure with shells and added colorful rosettes on the roof. Windows and a skylight add a practical touch.

A Breed Apart

The Gypsy Caravan
Ian and Katherine McGillivray
Toronto

Fully functional (just add horsepower), the Gypsy Caravan features everything the nomadic canine needs for years of happy roaming. The painted plywood shell is topped with a decorative copper roof (complete with chimney), and is punctuated by a stained-glass window depicting the resident vagabond sporting a rakish earring.

Architect Ian McGillivray and his teenage daughter, Katherine, collaborated on the project, which took about six weeks to build. Among the amenities: a barrel affixed to the side that can conceal a bowl of kibble.

Let Sleeping Dogs Lie
Jeanine Anderson Guncheon, John "Jandy" Anderson
Oak Park, Illinois

With his ferocious gaze and snaggletooth snarl, this cranky canine means business.

Art furniture makers Jeanine Anderson Guncheon and John "Jandy" Anderson created the piece for a show at the Dog Museum in Saint Louis. The rear of the doghouse features a carving of (what else?) the dog's rear end. The side is painted with a handy aphorism ("Don't bite the hand that feeds you"), while the interior just might be an homage to our thirty-seventh president and his favorite campaign companion, Checkers.

A Breed Apart

!!!*SIT*!!!
Bonnie Sachs
Los Angeles

Los Angeles interior designer Bonnie Sachs crafted this example of what she calls "Milkbone vernacular" after the death of her springer spaniel, Alfie. Left with some boxes of uneaten dog biscuits, she hot-glued the contents onto a wooden armature. Unfortunately, she ran a little short: the project took forty-six boxes to complete.

Brown biscuits form a "ruffsticated" foundation, while yellow, orange, tan, and red biscuits were layered like Spanish tiles on the roof. The carpet inside is an actual calico fabric adorned with spaniel heads. Furnishings are painted onto the walls alongside framed portraits of Alfie and other dogs.

Lassie
Come Home
Smart Design, LLC
New York

Man's best friend? For some it would be a toss-up between Rover
and the remote control.

Now there's no need to choose, thanks to New York product
designers Tucker Viemeister, Peter Stathis, Tom Dair, and Jurgen
Laub, who fashioned this creation from a vintage console TV.
Already equipped with its own picture window and ventilated
back, the doghouse just needed a corrugated fiberglass roof,
antenna, and avocado shag carpet (plus the obligatory
portrait of Timmy).

Notes Dair, "When you actually get a dog
in there it's kind of like watching *Lassie*."

The Soloist
Al Cimini and Joe Ventura
Stouffville, Ontario

Anyone for a polka? This accordion-player doghouse stands
six feet tall, and was a collaboration between interior designer
Al Cimini and artist Joe Ventura. The squeezebox is made from
rigid foam insulation covered with a rubber membrane. The face
is crafted from fiberglass over a wooden armature.

Chocolatier Brook Jones discovered the doghouse when
it was displayed at a Toronto mall. Today it sits at the edge of
a forest on her property outside Toronto.

"It's quite visible as you walk up the winding path
to the house," Brook says. "It takes the breath out
of you."

On the Road to Zanzibar
Huntsman Architectural Group
San Francisco

Designed by Mark Harbick and Linda Parker, this paisley pup tent rests on an armature of gilded dowels set upon a platform covered in 18-karat-gold paint. The removable top is trimmed with gold braid and crowned with a plume of ostrich feathers. Jeweled doggy dishes rest on a Persian runner leading to Tiger's pillow-filled chamber. A battery-powered chandelier lights the interior.

A Breed Apart

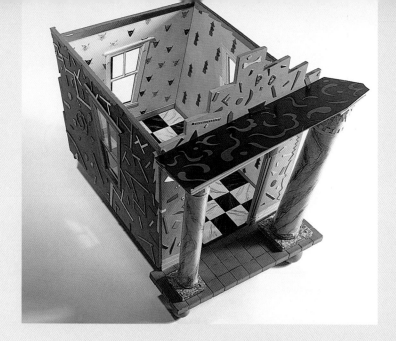

▲ Fido's Amazing Technicolor Dreamhouse
Tom Pfannerstill
Louisville, Kentucky

Artist Tom Pfannerstill's artfully askew confection features marbleized PVC columns in front and the kind of interior dogs dream of—literally. Bunnies, bones, cats, and fire hydrants dance across the walls, while a V-formation of geese skewers the azure ceiling.

Originally Pfannerstill designed the doghouse with a pitched roof. "Then I thought I might as well make it utilitarian, so I put a flat top on it," he says. The creation sits in his family room, where he uses it as a table.

"We have a very eclectic decor," concedes the artist.

Dog Cabin ➤
Mark Simon, Margaret Wazuka, Paul L. Shainberg
Essex, Connecticut

For an exhibit at the Cooper-Hewitt National Design Museum in New York, a team from Centerbrook Architects and Planners dipped seven hundred dog biscuits in polyester resin and applied them to a fiberglass-and-polyester shell. To form the roof, twenty-three dozen rawhide strips were soaked in water and flattened under weights. Then they were sealed with polyester resin and applied to the roof.

The design team soon discovered why dog biscuits never caught on as a building medium. "There was moisture on the inside," says participant Margaret Wazuka. "It started to smell."

Although dogs appreciated the aroma, humans were less tolerant. When the exhibit ended, the Dog Cabin had to be destroyed.

Reki
William M. Baxley, Vesa Loikas, Jose Solivas
Minneapolis

Stretching twelve feet in length, this cedar construction features removable Dacron walls and a slatted roof that directs rainwater into a gutter. The gutter empties into a trough, filling the wooden bowl at the end.

Owner Wendy Leo's dog, Jax, and daughter, Nicole, often play in the doghouse together. When Nicole crawls inside, Jax scampers up the ramp and stands guard over her.

Architect William M. Baxley of Frederick Bentz/Milo Thompson/Robert Rietow Inc. says the design was inspired by a dogsled. (Hence the name "Reki"—Finnish for "sled.") He liked the roofline so much, he plans to use a similar form on a Unitarian church he's designing.

The Muttropolitan Opera House. See page 81.

Puppourri

We scoured the country—from Central Bark West to Hollywoof and Vine—to come up with this outrageous array of doghouses. Each defies categorization, so we put them in a group all their own. The only thing they have in common is that they are all so uncommon. Enjoy!

The Trojan Dog
Lewis Davis and William H. Paxson
Ancramdale, New York

"They have a Trojan horse. Why not a Trojan dog?" reasoned architect Lewis Davis, who promptly remedied the situation with this four-foot-high creation designed for a charity auction. The architect's son, Michael Davis, painted the neo-Egyptian hieroglyphics that adorn the exterior (and bear the inscrutable inscription, "WOOF").

The doghouse didn't attract the kind of bidding Lewis felt it deserved, so he bought it himself and installed it on the porch of his country home.

"It's a nice companion," he says. "Everybody feels safe at night."

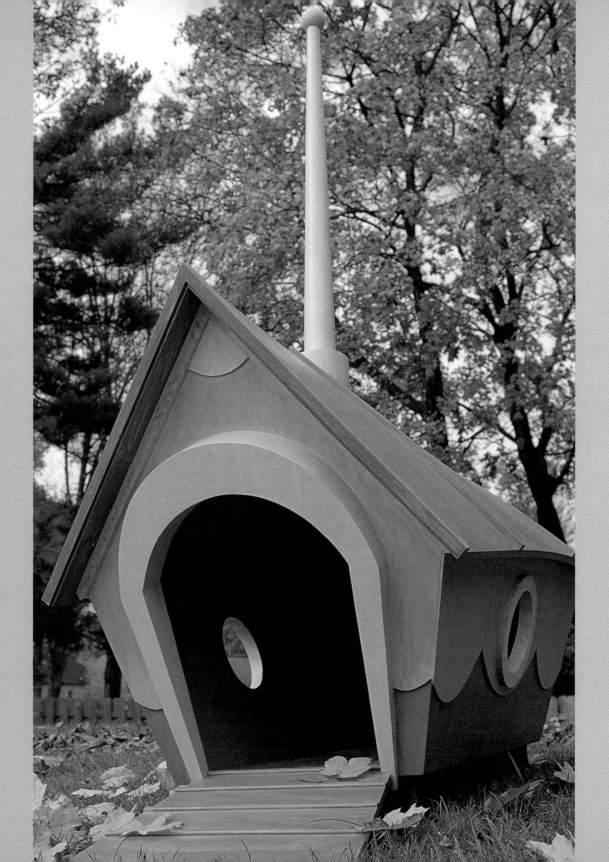

House for a Labrador Retriever

**Ellie Hays and
Matthew Moger, Lyman
S. A. Perry Architects
Stone Harbor, New Jersey**

With its bowed roof and forward-thrusting facade, this nautical doghouse appears poised to hit the surf. The designers, architect Ellie Hays and architectural designer Matthew Moger, were inspired by their boss's love of Labrador retrievers and that species's affection for water. The pair festooned the doghouse with cutout waves and porthole windows, and added a mast on top for good measure.

The doghouse was purchased by Perry and Diane Conte, but their Labrador, Otis, will not go near it. Perry enjoys the colorful creation just the same. "Our house has no character," he explains. "I guess that's one of the things that attracted me to the doghouse."

The
Pet à Porter
Gordon H Chong & Partners
San Francisco

You wouldn't dream of wearing the same outfit day after day. Why should your dog?

With Pet à Porter, you can change the look of your pet's abode quicker than you can say Donna Karan. The secret? A reversible slipcover (complete with matching cap and detachable dog bone) that slides over a PVC frame. In a flash your pet can go from a summery stripe to a sensible solid.

What's more, Pet à Porter folds down to fit in a convenient carrying case, so your pet will never be far from home.

The Muttropolitan
Opera House
Douglas W. Schmidt
San Francisco

What budding Muttzart or Poochini could resist his or her very own opera house? Especially one that comes with such an impeccable *petigree*?

Acclaimed scenic designer Douglas W. Schmidt and the crew from the San Francisco Opera's scenery and costume shops crafted this miniature stage set for a charity auction. The proscenium is framed with embroidered velvet trimmed with gold fringe, and is surrounded by hand-painted portraits of the aforementioned composers, as well as the somewhat more obscure "Engelbert Humperleg."

"The idea was to make it as much like stage scenery as possible," says Schmidt, who went so far as to stencil the "backstage" walls with names of various productions: *Corgi and Bess, Cosi fan Toto, Dog Giovanni, The Bartered Breed,* and, of course, *Tails of Hoffman.*

Puppourri

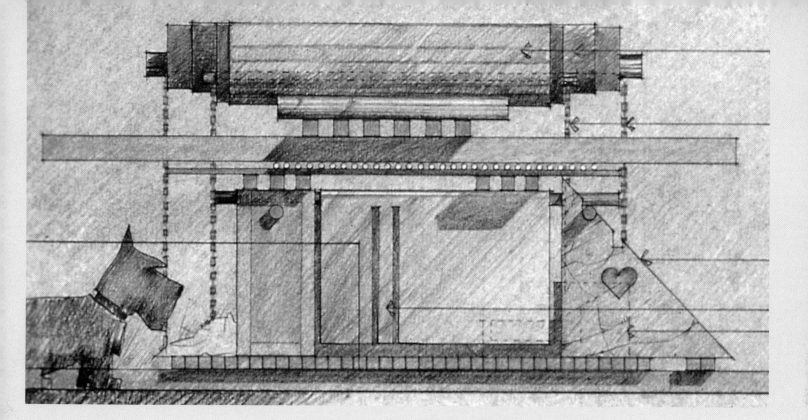

Garden Pavilion for Dave
J. Woodson Rainey Jr.
Arlington, Vermont

Architect J. Woodson Rainey Jr. gained notoriety a few years back for placing an eight-foot-square ant farm in the lobby of a Manhattan office building.

Turning his attention to dogs, Rainey designed this collection of cedar timbers, granite slabs and stainless-steel channels held together by gravity (making it easy to transport). Rain chains (inspired by Japanese architecture) drain roof water into a stone dish for the resident canine. The pet exits and enters through a leather flap built into the structure's side.

"I was trying to make something that didn't scream out 'doghouse,'" Rainey says.

No need to worry there. Visitors to Rainey's father-in-law's house in Vermont, where the doghouse resides, more often mistake it for a high-tech barbecue.

Puppourri

◄ The Hut Dog
Delta + design team,
CIBC Development Corporation
Toronto

This portable doghouse features a metal frame fitted with a waterproof polyester shell. The floor is raised off the ground to protect lawns and keep the occupant dry. The ears are pouches designed to hold dog food or playthings, while the cushioned tongue can be used inside or out. The nose is a detachable dog toy. The whole thing fits in a bag when not in use.

"I have seven nieces and nephews that *love* to play in it," says owner Fiona Taylor.

Apparently, adults are not immune to its allure, either. After a few of her parties, Taylor has woken to find adults sleeping inside.

◣ The Gate of Labs
Suter and Suter
Amagansett, New York

The portal into ancient Mycenae is flanked by a pair of carved lionesses—fearsome creatures designed to ward off unwanted intruders. Architects Richard and Bobette Suter had a more romantic notion in mind when they designed their own version, featuring a pair of smooching Labrador retrievers.

"I had Labs growing up," explains Bobette, who adorned the plywood exterior with real studded collars and furnished the interior with separate areas for dining and sleeping.

"People who see it are amused by it," remarks the owner.

Surely not the effect the Greeks had in mind.

The more I see of the representatives of the people, the more I admire my dogs.

WHY DOES A DOG BURY A BONE?   Dogma has nothing to do

"Who loves me, let him love my dog also.   - St. Bernard, 12th century   Why do dogs

Why do DOGS sometimes ROLL in Filth;   How sensitive is a dog's nose?   Sod Poodle is a coloquial name for th

Rover's
Rad Retreat

Mesher Shing & Associates
Seattle

This whimsical creation, dubbed "Rover's Rad Retreat" by
Seattle architects Mesher Shing & Associates, features a
corrugated-fiberglass roof that arches over a box trimmed
with galvanized metal. The side walls are embellished with
drawings of dogs, while the steps are inscribed with canine
aphorisms like "Dogma has nothing to do with dogs."
Owner Walter Parson's young daughter took to
the doghouse immediately, adding a door in front
so she could read or nap in private. Walter's
Bernese mountain dog, Carver, has yet
to venture inside.

Chuck and Lily's Campaign Tent
Robert Couturier
New York

To introduce their new novelty fabric, "Housepets," Donghia Textiles invited over a hundred architects and designers to create a pet object using the material. Among the winners: interior designer Robert Couturier's sumptuous campaign tent, designed for his Shih Tzus, Chuck and Lily.

Inspired by a garden folly at the Château de Grussay near Fontainebleau, the tent features a common sitting room and separate bedrooms for each dog.

Sadly, Couturier's creation was short-lived. The campaign tent was damaged in transit, leaving Chuck and Lily tentless but, one suspects, not homeless.

A Doghouse for Hobie and Ryely
J. Michael Holliday
Siesta Key, Florida

Architect J. Michael Holliday's whimsical take on Florida vernacular mixes practicality with *Miami Vice* verve. Custom-designed for western Florida's hot, humid weather, the open pavilion allows cooling breezes to pass right through, while the corrugated fiberglass roof protects golden retrievers Hobie and Ryely from torrential afternoon showers. The rear wall (equipped with surveillance window) shields the pets from prevailing winds. Since the direction of that wind changes seasonally, the doghouse can be easily moved (a safeguard against mildew in this tropical climate).

Directory of Designers

The doghouses in this book were created by the following architects, designers, and artists:

John "Jandy" Anderson
1842 115 Street
Chippewa Falls, WI 54729
715/834-1619

Babey Moulton
Jue & Booth
510 Third Street
San Francisco, CA 94107
415/979-9880

Frederick Bentz/
Milo Thompson/
Robert Rietow Inc.
2600 Foshay Tower
Minneapolis, MN 55402
612/332-1234

John Bowron Architects
75 Woodrow Avenue
Toronto, Ontario
M4C 1G3
CANADA
416/693-8680

Michael J. Brolly
343 West State Street
Hamburg, PA 19526
610/562-5119

BWBR Architects
400 Sibley Street,
Suite 500
Saint Paul, MN 55101
651/290-1880

Centerbrook Architects
and Planners
Box 955
Centerbrook, CT 06409
860/767-0175

Gordon H Chong &
Partners
130 Sutter Street,
Suite 300
San Francisco, CA 94104
415/433-0120

CIBC Development
Corporation
Commerce Court
21 Melinda Street
Fifth Floor CCE5
Toronto, Ontario M5L 1G4
CANADA
416/861-5100

Al Cimini
15 Frankdale Avenue
Toronto, Ontario M4J 3Z8
CANADA
416/463-6769

John M. Collins Historic
Building Design
36 Main Street
Roslyn, NY 11576
516/625-4060

Robert Couturier Inc.
138 West 25 St.,
11th Floor
New York, NY 10001
212/463-7177

Davis Brody Bond
Architects and Planners
315 Hudson Street
New York, NY 10013
212/633-4700

Ralph L. Duesing AIA
Architect
5207 McKinney Avenue,
Suite 11
Dallas, TX 75205
214/528-6750

Jeanine Anderson
Guncheon Studio
7316 Madison Street
Forest Park, IL 60130
708/366-2360

Gwathmey Siegel &
Associates Architects
475 Tenth Avenue
New York, NY 10018
212/947-1240

Haigh Architects
125 Greenwich Avenue
Greenwich, CT 06830
203/869-5445

Stefan Hastrup
451 Fulton Street
San Francisco, CA 94102
415/431-8044

Jarrett Hedborg
Interior Design
8811 Alden Drive,
Suite 11
Los Angeles, CA 90048
310/271-1437

Holey Associates
2 South Park
Third Floor
San Francisco, CA 94107
415/537-0999

J. Michael Holliday
DesignARC
1 North Calle Cesar
Chavez Street, #210
Santa Barbara, CA 93103
805/963-4401

Huntsman
Architectural Group
465 California Street,
Suite 1000
San Francisco, CA 94104
415/394-1212

Doug Kelbaugh, FAIA
College of Architecture
& Urban Planning
University of Michigan
2000 Bonisteel Boulevard
Ann Arbor, MI 48109
734/764-1315

Hely Lima
5 Riverside Drive
New York, NY 10023
212/799-1058

Ian McGillivray
McGillivray—Architect
416 Moore Avenue,
Suite 103
Toronto, Ontario M4G 1C9
CANADA
416/425-9298

Mesher Shing & Associates
506 Second Avenue
Suite 3300
Seattle, WA 98104
206/622-4981

Mark Millett
Millett Associates
117 Summit Avenue East
Seattle, WA 98102
206/325-0646

NBBJ Architecture
Design and Planning
130 Sutter Street,
Second Floor
San Francisco, CA 94104
415/981-1100

Jeff Oesterle
Oest Metalworks
1230A East Jackson Street
Pheonix, AZ 85034
602/256-7567

Lyman S. A. Perry
Architects
42 Cassatt Avenue
Berwyn, PA 19312
610/889-9966

Tom Pfannerstill
2334 Alta Avenue
Louisville, KY 40205
502/583-9154

Antoine Predock Architect
529 Victoria Avenue
Venice, CA 90291
310/577-4656

J. Woodson Rainey Jr., AIA
192 Lexington Avenue
New York, NY 10016
212/686-4576

Terry Russell
1139 Charter Oak
Parkway
Saint Louis, MO 63146
314/997-2574

Bonnie Sachs
311 Bora Bora Way,
Suite 305
Marina del Rey, CA 90292
310/306-4595

Norman B. Sandler
1000 Lenora Street,
Suite 400
Seattle, WA 98121
206/682-5211

Douglas W. Schmidt
9 Roosevelt Way
San Francisco, CA 94114
415/864-1486

Senior Rae
Architecture + Art
1230A East Jackson Street
Phoenix, AZ 85034
602/256-2622

Stuart Silk Architects
80 Vine Street
Seattle, WA 98121
206/728-9500

Smart Design, LLC
137 Varick Street
New York, NY 10013
212/807-8150

Smith and Thompson
Architects
542 Cathedral Parkway
New York, NY 10025
212/865-0151

Suter and Suter
PO Box 389
East Moriches, NY 11940
516/878-4602

Joe Ventura
80 Plewes Road
Toronto, Ontario
M3K 1K7
CANADA
905/660-1926

Barbara K. Westover
5929 Acacia Avenue
Oakland, CA 94618
510/653-9284

The Frank Lloyd Wright
Foundation
Taliesin West
PO Box 4430
Scottsdale, AZ 85261
602/860-2700

Acknowledgments

A heartfelt thanks to all those who helped with the production of this book:

Yosh Asato, AIA San Francisco / Hope Kingsbury, Hazelton Lanes Shopping Centre / Craig Kitt, Animal Rescue Fund of the Hamptons, Inc. / Jeffrey Golick, Abbeville Press / Angela Miller / Nancy Carlisle / Katherine Grier / John Mihaly / Aarne Anton / Robert Reeves / Historic Hudson Valley, Tarrytown, New York / Pals for Life / Joel Kimmel / PAWS/LA / Dove Lewis Emergency Animal Hospital / Ted Degener / *Dog Fancy* magazine / Seattle Public Library / Margo Stipe, The Frank Lloyd Wright Archives / Donghia / Sonet Agency Ltd. / Chuck Hudson / Allen Fisher, Lyndon B. Johnson Library / Marilyn Morrison, Ronald Reagan Library / Valerie Kremer, Kentucky Art and Craft Foundation / Mark Sheppard / . . . and all the doghouse owners. **Special thanks to Susan Urstadt, whose support and enthusiasm made this project possible.**

Illustration and Photography Credits

Robert Anderson: back cover (top left), 30, 48 / Atlanta Humane Society: 11 / Jonathan Barber: 82 / Adam Bartos: 1, 74, 96 / Dick Busher: 86 / Rik Clingerman: 2, 45 / Ted Degener: 55 / Alan Ferguson: 90, 91 / Polly Friedlander: 24, 46 / Robert A. Fryer: 76, 77 / Peter Gabor: 84 / Bruce Gibson: 27, 56, 57, 65 / David W. Haas: 47 / Paul Haigh: 42, 43 / Alec Harrison, courtesty of Donghia: 89 / Historic Hudson Valley, Tarrytown, N.Y.: 9 / Oliver Kienzi: 34 / John Lair Studio: 50, 68 / Michael Lyon: 22 / Jan Marie Mackin: 36 / Gary Mankus: 3, 59 / Joshua McHugh: 15 / Alex McLean: 12, 29, 85 / The Metropolitan Museum of Art, gift of Mr. and Mrs. Charles Wrightsman, 1971, (1971.206.18): 8 / Ganesh Nayak: 49 / PAWS/LA: 23, 60 / J. Woodson Rainey Jr.: 6, 83 / Sharon Risedorph: front cover, back cover (bottom left), 20, 35, 52, 54, 67, 72, 78, 80 / Bonnie Sachs: 61 / Claudio Santini: 38, 39 / Douglas W. Schmidt: endpapers / Michael Seidl Photography: 16 / Ken Skalski: 62 / William Allin Storrer: 41 / Brian Vanden Brink: back cover (bottom right), 10 / Margaret Wazuka: back cover (top right), 69 / Wilsonart: 18 / Don F. Wong: 70 / Frank Lloyd Wright drawings are Copyright © 1998 The Frank Lloyd Wright Foundation, Scottsdale, Ariz.: 40 / William P. Wright: 33 / Ed Zealy: 19

Editor:
Jeffrey
Golick

Designer:
Jennifer
O'Connor

Production
Director:
Hope
Koturo

First edition
4 6 8 10 9 7 5

Library of Congress Cataloging-in-Publication Data
Albert, Fred.
Barkitecture / by Fred Albert. — 1st ed.
p.   cm.
ISBN 0-7892-0373-1
1. Doghouses—Exhibitions.   I. Title.
SF427.43.A58   1999
728'.9—dc21   98-46089

We have been unable to identify the owners of the doghouses
pictured on pages 41, 42, 60, 78, and 90. If you have any
information about these projects, please contact
Abbeville Press, 22 Cortlandt Street,
New York, N.Y. 10007.

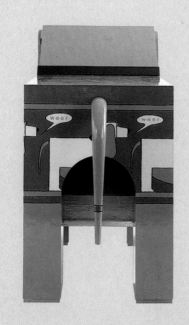

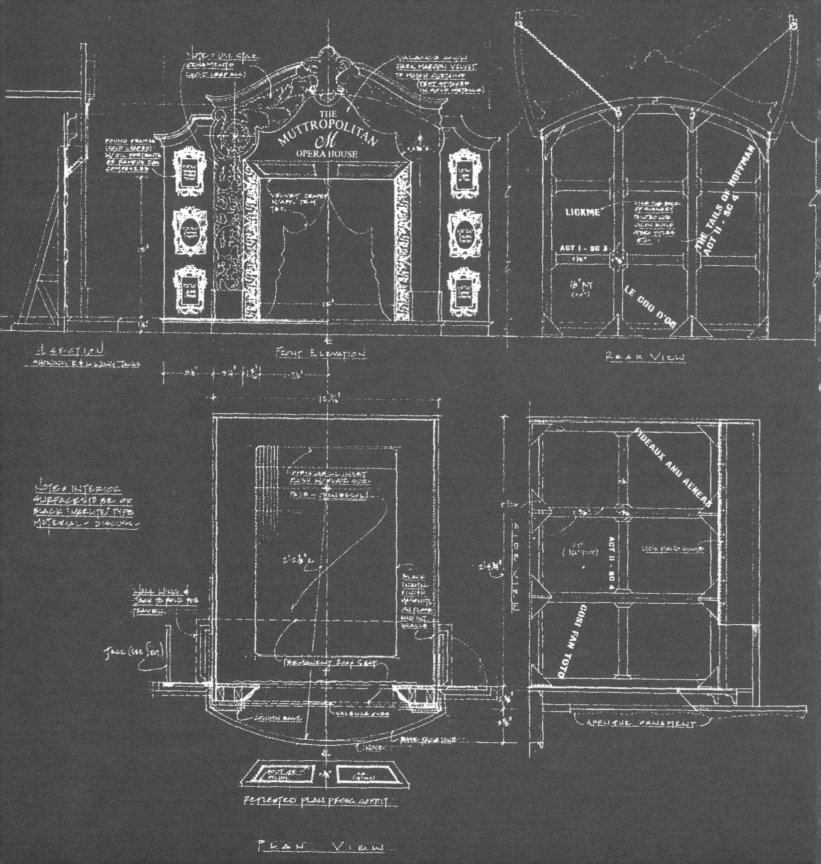